Made in the USA
Monee, IL
17 March 2022

93027234R00069